COMMON ENGLISH OPPOSITES FOR KIDS

Let's Start Learning
Together Opposites

VOL 1

Boy
Is the
Opposite
Of !!!
?

Boy

Big
Is the Opposite Of !!!
?

Big
Is The Opposite Of
Small

Adult
Is the Opposite Of !!!
?

Adult

Active
Is the Opposite Of !!!
?

Active

Beautiful
Is the Opposite Of !!!
?

Beautiful

Fat
Is the Opposite Of !!!
?

Fat
Slim
Is The Opposite Of

Good
Is the
Opposite
Of !!!
?

Good
Is The Opposite Of
Bad
DON'T SMOKE

Teacher
Is the Opposite Of !!!
?

Teacher

Man
Is the Opposite Of !!!
?

Man

Woman

Tall
Is the Opposite Of !!!
?

Tall
Is The Opposite Of
Small

Fast
Is the
Opposite
Of !!!
?

Fast

Slow

Ceiling
Is the Opposite Of !!!
?

Ceiling

Clean
Is the
Opposite
Of !!!
?

Clean

Cheap
Is the Opposite Of !!!
?

Cheap
Expensive
Is The Opposite Of

9 798673 455920